IMAGES
of America

LYNDON B. JOHNSON
NATIONAL HISTORICAL PARK

The LBJ Ranch is the premier highlight of Lyndon B. Johnson National Historical Park. Known as the "Texas White House," it gained worldwide recognition as one of the most famous ranches in the United States. The ranch has been open for tours since 1973. After the death of Lady Bird Johnson in 2007, the National Park Service began to return the interior of the Texas White House to its mid- to late-1960s appearance. Since August 2008, on what would have been Pres. Lyndon Johnson's 100th birthday, park staff opened the president's office as the first public section of the house. The grand opening of all public areas of Pres. Lyndon and Lady Bird Johnson's gift to the American people takes place in 2012. After the first floor of the ranch house is opened, the National Park Service will begin restoration of the second floor. (Courtesy of the Lyndon B. Johnson National Historical Park.)

ON THE COVER: This photograph of (from left to right) Luci, Lynda, Lady Bird, and then-senator Lyndon Johnson was taken on the LBJ Ranch in September 1954. (Courtesy of the LBJ Library and Museum.)

IMAGES
of America

LYNDON B. JOHNSON
NATIONAL HISTORICAL PARK

Kelly Carper Polden and
the Lyndon B. Johnson National Historical Park
Foreword by Lynda Johnson Robb

ARCADIA
PUBLISHING

Published by Arcadia Publishing
Charleston, South Carolina

Printed in the United States of America

Library of Congress Control Number: 2010935615

For all general information, please contact Arcadia Publishing:
Telephone 843-853-2070
Fax 843-853-0044
E-mail sales@arcadiapublishing.com
For customer service and orders:
Toll-Free 1-888-313-2665

Visit us on the Internet at www.arcadiapublishing.com

I dedicate this book to my maternal grandmother, Lucille Wass Holmberg, who was a lifelong creative writing mentor, and to my mother, Marilyn Louise Holmberg Carper, who has always provided me with love and encouragement to pursue my passions and goals in life.

The front (facing south) of the Lyndon B. Johnson Library and Museum in Austin, Texas, is pictured. (Courtesy of the LBJ Library and Museum.)

CONTENTS

Lynda Johnson Robb (left) and her sister, Luci Johnson, were photographed at the LBJ Ranch Hangar in April 2009 to attend the annual "Reflections of the '60s, an LBJ Ranch" special event. (Courtesy of Russ Whitlock.)

From left to right, Lynda, Lady Bird, Luci, and Congressman Lyndon Johnson await voting results from the 1948 primary election following Johnson's campaign for the U.S. Senate. (Courtesy of the LBJ Library and Museum.)

FOREWORD

Many people have asked my sister, Luci, and me how we felt the day we found out that Mother and Daddy had deeded the LBJ Ranch to the National Park Service. We probably had an idea that it may happen; after all, Daddy had already donated to the people of America his childhood home and the ancestral structures and properties of the first Johnson settlers in the Texas Hill Country.

Daddy wanted future generations to experience the rural landscapes, small towns, and lifeways of his hill country family and neighbors. What he learned as a child and young man growing up in a rural setting influenced many elements of his "Great Society" legislation. Mother had grown up in the small town of Karnack, in east Texas, so she, too, treasured the rural experience of knowing all of your neighbors.

As first lady, Mother crisscrossed the nation promoting the restoration of public places, the creation of parks, and reminding her fellow citizens of the natural beauty contained within America's borders. Daddy certainly felt her influence and responded by signing more national parks bills than any other president. When Mother pushed for a program to beautify the nation's roadways, Daddy worked his legislative magic with Congress and the 1965 Highway Beautification Bill became law. This law, as with so many others dealing with civil rights, voting rights, equal opportunity, arts and humanities, improved health and working conditions, and education created during Daddy's administration, continues to benefit Americans today.

The National Park Service likes to say the national historical park incorporates a "circle of life" that begins with Daddy's birth and continues for 64 years until his 1973 death in the ranch house. No other presidential park holds as many historic structures significant to a president's life. Most folks think of Daddy in relation to the Texas White House and the LBJ Ranch. Certainly they are the main focus of the park, but there is so much more to the story.

In a small, wood-framed, dogtrot-style house, a baby boy was born in August 1908. Family folklore says his father mounted a horse and rode throughout the countryside announcing the birth of his first child. Sam E. Johnson Jr. probably stopped under the live oak that shaded the stone house owned by his sister and brother-in-law to share the news of his son's birth.

As a child, Daddy could walk a few hundred yards from his family's house to visit his grandparents. I expect he heard stories told by his grandfather of the cattle drives from their frontier cabin in what is now Johnson City. As a child, he learned of the family's history surviving the Texas frontier. His grandparents, like so many others, were drawn to the hill country by the clear, year-round, flowing rivers and streams, the tall grasses swaying in the wind, and the preponderance of live oaks providing shade from the hot summer sun. What they found over time was thin soil, Native Americans zealous to protect their lands, and often-inclement weather. But this deceiving landscape would not conquer the hardy souls who settled the hill country, and their descendants still live, work, and protect these beloved lands.

During the good years of the cattle trade in the 1870s, Daddy's second cousin, James Polk Johnson, was so wealthy he donated the original land to create a community and build Johnson City's bank, hotel, and saloon. The townsfolk, in gratitude for his gift, named their community Johnson City. There was a time when Daddy's ancestors were the largest landowners in Blanco County, but all that would change with a drop in the market and a string of bad weather events.

Daddy was born in Gillespie County but only lived there five years before his parents moved the growing family into a home in Blanco County's Johnson City. The house remains today, maintained in its 1920s appearance that Daddy would have known in his youth. From the front porch of that house, candidate Lyndon Johnson announced his run for a seat in the House of Representatives. There are photographs taken that night in 1935. When I look at the expression on Mother's face I see support and excitement tempered with some hesitation and concern. In one of Mother's early letters to Daddy, she expresses her concern that he may want to go into politics. "Indeed it was politics." Mother would become the gracious and generous wife of a congressman, senator, vice president, and president.

As Daddy's role in the House of Representatives and the Senate increased, we were removed from the hill country for long periods of time. The tug of home never was far from Daddy's heart, and in 1951 he jumped at the chance to purchase Aunt Frank Martin's house. I'm sure Mother was a great deal less enthusiastic when Daddy excitedly shared the news that Aunt Frank was going to sell the old house and 200 acres of land. Mother wasn't looking forward to raising two daughters and renovating an old house that had fallen into disrepair over the years.

My life at the LBJ Ranch was spent during summers, school holidays, and whenever Daddy could get free from Washington. For two years, in 1952 and 1953, we lived at the ranch while Congress was out of session. I went to school in Johnson City. I learned to play marbles on the playground dirt and made friends in the area. My father's first cousin Ava Cox taught first grade. In the 1952 flood, I couldn't get back across the river and had to stay with her in Johnson City until the river went down. Going to a rural school was an enlightening experience that gave me a taste of Daddy's childhood.

Daddy was becoming increasingly influential in Washington and his role as senate majority leader required that he spend even more time at the Capitol. With ever-improving air travel, we were able to make more frequent trips to the LBJ Ranch, first landing on a grass runway and later on an asphalt airstrip that got longer as official visitation to the ranch increased.

Throughout the balance of Daddy's political career, the world would become familiar with LBJ Ranch. Mother and Daddy both enjoyed entertaining and being surrounded by friends and family. I always enjoyed watching the local folks of Johnson City and Stonewall mix and mingle with world leaders at the very popular barbecues held on the ranch. I have no doubt that Daddy much preferred a good barbecue in the oak grove to any formal head-of-state dinner in Washington. On the ranch, his pace never slowed, but he could be more relaxed when he was surrounded by family in the place he loved. When the world went into shock and mourning over President Kennedy's assassination, LBJ Ranch fell quiet as well. Before the horrible news came from Dallas, the ranch had been a flurry of activity in preparation for the president and first lady's pending visit. There were to be press conferences, a barbecue, horse rides and hunts for relaxation, and of course a personal guided tour of LBJ Ranch by Daddy.

Daddy didn't want to travel or go on vacation to anywhere other than LBJ Ranch. Mother often said, "all the world is welcome," and certainly the world got to know the ranch and Texas White House between 1963 and 1969. The news agencies first coined the phrase "Texas White House," and the name stuck.

I hope you enjoy this compilation of photographs that span almost a century of time. Daddy was proud of his hill country roots and took great pride in the genuine people who inhabited the region. My sister, Luci, is fond of saying that Daddy loved the people of the hill country, "people who cared when you were sick and knew when you died."

To answer the opening question: Luci and I felt surprise and disappointment that Mother and Daddy would give away these places that meant so much to our grandchildren and us. But Mother and Daddy were giving and caring for the people around them and the citizens of the nation for most of their lives. Mother was fond of a set of pillows on her bed that read, "I slept and dreamed of beauty, I awoke and found life was duty." Today we miss the family home, a place that Mother continued to enjoy with generations of Johnsons until her death in 2007. That said, the descendants of Lyndon and Lady Bird Johnson honor their requests and are thrilled that the National Park Service is fulfilling our parents' dream to share the important stories, life, and legacy of the 36th president of the United States and his Lady Bird Johnson.

Enjoy!

—Lynda Johnson Robb

ACKNOWLEDGMENTS

Many of the staff members at Lyndon B. Johnson National Historical Park provided assistance with photographs and information for this book, including park superintendent Russ Whitlock and his always-resourceful assistant Bonnie Jenschke, park chief of interpretation and resource management Gus Sanchez, and park curator Virginia Kilby. A very special thank you goes to park archivist Bao Nguyen for her expertise with the photo archives and her much-appreciated photo technician skills. Special thanks also to LBJ Library and Museum staff members Kristen Lambert, for her invaluable assistance with photographic research, and Charles Bogel, for being a top-notch photo technician. Unless otherwise noted, photographs were provided courtesy of the archives at Lyndon B. Johnson National Historical Park, headquartered in Johnson City, Texas, and the LBJ Library and Museum in Austin, Texas. Numerous photographers served Lyndon Johnson, including Fred Mang, Yoichi Okamoto, Kevin Smith, Art Kowert, Frank Wolfe, Mike Geissinger, and Robert Knudsen.

Thank you to Kristie Kelly and Hannah Carney of Arcadia for the support, advice, and much-appreciated feedback provided during the writing of this book.

This book would not be possible without the love and dedication of my husband, Howard, as well as support from friends and family.

INTRODUCTION

No one could ever understand Lyndon Johnson unless they understood the land and the people from which he came. . . . Here on these familiar hills under these expansive skies and under these oak trees that he loved so much, his life has come full circle. . . . His roots were deep in the Texas Hill Country.

—Rev. Billy Graham

The National Park Service is charged with preserving unique places throughout the United States. Such is the case with Lyndon B. Johnson National Historical Park, which is dedicated to the 36th president of the United States and holds more structures and landscapes significant to an American president than any other site in the country. The park represents Lyndon Johnson's full circle of life, from birthplace to final resting place, from his heritage to his legacy.

Pres. Lyndon B. Johnson took great pride in his heritage and the Texas Hill Country roots set down by his pioneer ancestors. He delighted in showing guests the ancestral settlement, as well as his birthplace, boyhood home, and the family treasure—the LBJ Ranch and the home that became known as the Texas White House. In a magnanimous gesture, Lyndon and Lady Bird Johnson gifted these cherished assets to the people of the United States. Lady Bird Johnson often spoke of her husband's generosity and his need to be surrounded by people. The gift of his ranch and family property to the American people is an LBJ legacy, a lasting gesture of his gracious character.

This book about Lyndon B. Johnson National Historical Park will provide visitors, future visitors, friends, and guests with a comprehensive understanding of this American treasure, told through a vast collection of photographs and vignettes that capture the unique significance of Lyndon B. Johnson and his generous spirit. Images illustrate the rich history of the national park property and include Johnson family photographs exemplifying the calming impact the LBJ Ranch had on the president, his family, and a host of national and global dignitaries who visited the Texas White House.

Lyndon Johnson is considered by many to have been the most influential president to date. President Johnson combined his many years of experience in Washington with consummate political skills to effectively push through sweeping legislation that completely changed the United States. It is fitting that Lyndon B. Johnson National Historical Park, located at the crossroads of the Texas Hill Country in Johnson City just an hour west of the Texas capital of Austin, preserves and shares the places that so influenced a young LBJ and continued to influence many of his decisions throughout his life. These places were a sanctuary, a source of inspiration and renewal for Lyndon Johnson and his family. This land was the setting for more than one-quarter of his five-year presidency and is now his final resting place.

Located within the boundaries of the park is the cabin his paternal grandparents lived in when they migrated to Blanco County and began to deal in the emerging Texas cattle industry. The replica of the home in which he was born was reconstructed by LBJ from memory and photographs. In Johnson City, his boyhood home preserves the house where he and four siblings grew into young adulthood, influenced by a small dusty agricultural community of Johnson City, a college educated mother, and a Texas state representative father who frequently held political meetings at the house. Of course, one of the most defining sites for President Johnson was the LBJ Ranch and the Texas White House.

Throughout Lyndon and Lady Bird Johnson's public life, they invited the world to dine, visit, relax, meet, and consult on the issues of the day. From 1951—when the Johnsons purchased the ranch and house from Lyndon's aunt Frank Martin—through Lady Bird's death in 2007, the entire world was welcome. Today the Western National Parks Association—with great assistance from the Friends of LBJ National Park, the LBJ Library and Museum, former members of the Johnson administration, and, of course, the Johnson family—are preserving and caring for these places once owned by the 36th president and his wife. Restoration of the Texas White House will be completed by late 2011 with a grand opening planned in spring 2012, in time for the blooming of Lady Bird Johnson's beloved Texas wildflowers and her 100th birthday celebration.

Lady Bird Johnson and Lyndon Johnson enjoy a moment of solitude, seated in a field of wildflowers on the LBJ Ranch.

One

THE JOHNSON SETTLEMENT

*It was once a barren land. The angular hills were covered with scrub cedar and a
few live oaks. Little would grow in the harsh caliche soil. And each spring the Pedernales
River would flood the valley. But men came and worked and endured and built.*

—Lyndon Baines Johnson

The land that is now part of the Lyndon B. Johnson National Historical Park is rich with history. It was home to many Native American tribes and cultures, including the Apache, Tonkawa, and Comanche. It experienced ethnic influences, including those from Spanish and German cultures. In 1721, Spanish explorers first crossed what is now called the Blanco (Spanish for "white") River. The Spaniards launched several campaigns against the Apaches in areas now known as Blanco and Gillespie Counties. Explorer Bernardo de Miranda is believed to have searched for mineral deposits in the area in 1756. Pedro Vial, a Frenchman in Spanish service who was selected to "blaze a more direct route between San Antonio and Santa Fe," according to National Park Service employee E. C. Bearss, crossed into what is now Blanco County in 1786. The Spanish explorers named the Pedernales River for its abundant flint along the riverbanks. For nearly 60 years after these recorded Spanish explorations, the area that became known as the Johnson Settlement was a wild and untamed land. A wave of German immigrants arrived in the region by the 1840s, settling mainly in areas to the south and west of Blanco County, and had a profound impact on building design and land use throughout the Texas Hill Country.

Blanco County was formed in 1856, the same year that James Provost and his wife purchased 320 acres of the Joseph Duel land grant that includes present day Johnson City and the Johnson Settlement. Provost built a log cabin with a stone fireplace and several modest outbuildings. By 1864, Lyndon Johnson's grandfather, Sam Ealy Johnson Sr., lived on the acreage in the Provost log cabin but did not hold title to the land. Sam and his brother Jesse Thomas "Tom" Johnson acquired the property on December 8, 1869. It soon became the headquarters for the brothers' vast cattle business.

Today many of the original Johnson Settlement structures have been saved and renovated to their 1860s appearance, enabling visitors to step back in time and experience the heritage of Lyndon Johnson.

Some of the first herds of cattle were trailed from Texas in 1866 along the Shawnee Trail to the railhead at Sedalia, Missouri. As the railhead moved westward, drovers sent cowboys and cattle on various trails, including the Chisholm Trail to Abilene, Kansas. Sam Johnson Sr. and his brother Tom made their first cattle drive in 1867. They bought the cattle on credit, and when they returned in the fall, they paid for the cattle in gold. Cattle valued at $2 per head in Texas were sold for $10 apiece at the railhead. As the market demand increased, cattle were sold at the railhead for up to $40 per head. In 1870, Tom and Sam Johnson and their hired cowboys had driven 7,000 head of cattle to the railhead in Kansas. This photograph is of a Johnson brothers cattle drive around 1870 that originated in Blanco County. The only identified cowboy, based on a handwritten note on the original photograph, is John Stribling, who is the third cowboy from the left.

Two cowboys who worked for the Johnson brothers prepare to brand a steer on the open prairie. Cattle brands are an important aspect of America's "cattle kingdom" heritage and tradition. Brands were stamped onto an animal's hide using a hot iron forged into the shape of the owner's brand. Another branding technique was known as a "running brand" where a hot poker or other tool was used to "draw" an image on the animal's hide. Rustlers often used a running brand to disfigure the original brand.

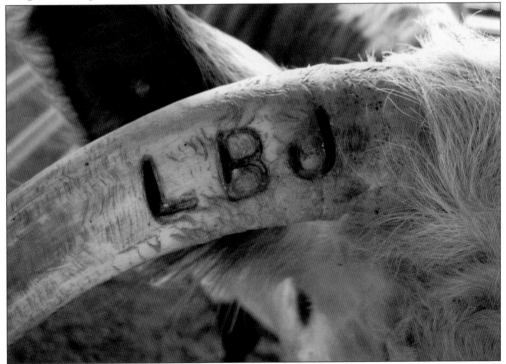

Ranch owners registered brands as a way to keep cattle and horse thieves at bay and to identify stock. In 1951, Lyndon Johnson registered a brand that was reportedly used by his grandfather. The brand continues to be used today and is known as the BarJBar or "— J —." He also used a brand with his well-recognized initials, LBJ.

After the brothers' successful first cattle drive, Sam married Eliza Bunton of Lockhart, Texas, on December 11, 1867, and moved to Blanco County, where they set up a home in what is now known as the Johnson Settlement. Over time, the couple added on to the cabin toward the east, creating the dogtrot breezeway between the original Provost section and the Johnson addition. Sam Sr. bought Tom's interest in the ranch, paying $1,200 for Tom's share in 1869.

Tom and Sam Johnson had the largest trail driving operation in Blanco and the surrounding counties. Pictured here, a group of cowboys pose near one of the Johnson brothers' many cattle pens prior to a roundup. Charles Klett, a member of a pioneer Blanco County family, worked as a cowboy for the Johnsons. He said the Johnsons built sprawling pens and corrals that stretched from the headquarters toward the Pedernales River, virtually covering the present site of Johnson City. The Johnson brothers used the area now known as the Johnson Settlement as headquarters for their cattle operation. They were better known as drovers rather than ranchers in those early days, because rather than raising the cattle, they rounded up wild cattle or bought cattle on credit to be sold at far-flung railheads.

Cowboys pose with their horses while in town to pick up supplies. Cowboy A. W. Capt joined the Johnson cattle roundups in 1870. His experience was later captured in *Trail Drivers of Texas*, a 1925 book compiled by J. Marvin Hunter and printed by Cokesbury Press. Capt recalled, "The roundup or range hands and range boss usually gathered, road branded and delivered a herd of from 2,500 to 3,000 head of cattle, which a trail boss and his outfit received at headquarters ranch, but sometimes we delivered them at the Seven Live Oaks on the prairie west of Austin. After a good night's rest, the ranch hands, bidding their relief 'so long, we'll meet you later in Kansas,' with pack and ponies, hit the back trails for another herd for the next outfit." In 1870, the Johnson brothers and their cowboys drove an estimated 7,000 cattle northward and received $100,000. The brothers became significant participants in what became known as the "cattle kingdom" of Texas, helping to create the myth and legend of the Texas cowboy.

Before returning to Texas from a cattle drive, Tom and Sam Johnson usually bought several mules to sell or use as pack animals; mules were used as pack animals or as work animals. A period actor demonstrates how a mule skinner handled teams of mules that were used to till the soil for crop production.

Someone who works with or drives mules is known as a "mule skinner." This mule-skinner actor calls for park guests to join him on a special tour.

Teams of mules were often used to pull wagons, transporting both goods and people across the Texas Hill Country.

Congressman Lyndon Johnson, left, looks on as uncle Berry Roebuck shows Lynda Johnson where her great-grandmother Eliza Bunton Johnson hid under the house during an Indian raid. At times, the Johnson cattle drives were interrupted by Indian attacks along the trail. At the cabin, Eliza became accustomed to living with the constant threat of Indian attacks. She was always on the lookout for Indians approaching the home. She would take the children and hide beneath the log cabin, holding a diaper over the baby's mouth to prevent the child from crying out. During one attack, known as the battle of Deer Creek and located very near the Johnson home, three men were wounded and brought to the cabin for care. The Deer Creek event was too close for comfort, and Sam Sr. sent Eliza and the children back to Caldwell County to stay with family members. During this time, a baby girl named Frank Barnett Johnson was born. Frank would later become owner of what is now LBJ Ranch.

A period actor demonstrates what it was like to cook in the late 1860s, using the cabin fireplace. After Eliza Bunton Johnson returned from Caldwell County in 1870, she and Sam Sr. moved from the log cabin. They lived in Hays County for a period of time and later settled in Gillespie County in what is now part of the LBJ Ranch. Sam continued to be involved in the cattle business. The Johnson brothers expanded their cattle operation, sending herds up the trail in the early 1870s, but the business collapsed in late 1872. Due to a nationwide financial panic, their speculative risks caught up with them. Financial pressure was so great that the Johnsons were unable to sell their cattle at the railhead that year and had to winter them on the Kansas plains. They lost heavily in both cattle and money. Tom, who seemed to be the top man in the operation, was forced to sacrifice some choice real estate as many people suffered during the crisis. By 1873, Tom was in financial ruin. He left Blanco County but drove cattle for other outfits. On March 12, 1877, Tom drowned while moving a trail herd at the Kimball crossing on the Brazos River near Kopperl, Texas, in Bosque County.

Sam Sr. sold his Blanco County property for $4,000 on January 17, 1872, to his nephew James Polk Johnson, who would become the founder of Johnson City. Ten years later, on June 20, 1882, James sold the property for $3,000 to John Bruckner, who, in 1884 constructed the large Pennsylvania Dutch–style barn that still stands at the Johnson Settlement site. The James Polk Johnson barn has vertical slits that resemble rifle ports for fighting Indians or other invaders. Because of these slits, many believed that the buildings were used as fortresses, and many refer to them as the "Johnson forts." However, these slits are based on a German-style construction that provides ventilation while the thick walls provide protection from extreme heat or cold.

Volunteers and period actors take a short walk from the James Polk Johnson barn toward the Bruckner barn. The James Polk Johnson barn was mainly used as a horse shelter and currently is home to several horses.

John Bruckner acquired the Johnson property from James Polk Johnson, a nephew of Sam Sr. and the founder of Johnson City. The Bruckner family poses in front of the Provost-Johnson-Bruckner log cabin around 1911. At the time of Bruckner's death in 1931, the ranch consisted of 1,640 acres, with 125 acres under cultivation and the remainder as grazing land.

The Johnson Settlement features many Texas longhorn cattle, representative of the breed that LBJ's ancestors drove up the trail nearly 150 years ago. Texas longhorn almost became extinct, but in 1927, the U.S. Forest Service and several dedicated Texans saved the breed. The longhorn has a revered place in Texas and American history. The "cattle kingdom" that began in the late 1860s boomed and waned for more than four decades. During that time, an estimated 10 million cattle were driven along the trails from Texas to the northern railheads in Kansas and Missouri. An over-stimulation of cattle production in the late 1880s and changes in the cattle industry and market caused the final decline. By 1893, a severe drought and another nationwide panic put an end to the era, but the "cattle kingdom" and its cowboys—including the ancestors of Lyndon Baines Johnson—left an indelible mark on Texas that still lingers today, eliciting great pride and respect for the ranching way of life.

Period actors "rustle up a mess of vittles" during a reenactment of a cowboy chuck wagon. The chuck wagon was a cowboy's best friend on the trail. The typical chuck wagon was used to store cowboy bed rolls and personal items as well as a large supply of food, cooking utensils, and other daily items needed during long cattle drives.

Not long after President Johnson retired from office, the National Park Service, using funds donated by LBJ's family, purchased the Johnson Settlement area and reconstructed the remaining buildings that serve as a testament to the courage and resolve of the Johnson family and of Texas's early settlers. The original Provost-Johnson-Bruckner log cabin was carefully restored in the early 1970s.

During the reconstruction of the log cabin, the National Park Service was careful to use hand-hewn cedar shakes for the roof in an attempt to have the log cabin appear as it would have in the 1860s.

The Bruckner barn was built in 1884. Stone was quarried in the hills to the south of what is now the Johnson Settlement and was hauled by ox-pulled carts. The workmen who constructed the barn were the same crews that a year later built the Jim Johnson building, which once housed the Blanco County Courthouse and now is home to Johnson City Bank. This photograph of the barn was taken in 1972, prior to reconstruction.

On March 20, 1971, Fred Bruckner—John Bruckner's oldest son, who was born in November 1883—provided his recollections of the log cabin and enabled the National Park Service to restore the home to its original appearance.

A period actor demonstrates how to wash clothes using a washboard in a large wooden bucket filled with water that had to be heated over the fireplace.

The dogtrot-style cabin was constructed of squared logs that required chinking. A metal roof had been installed in 1911, but the National Park Service restored the cabin to its original appearance using traditional 19th-century-style cedar shingles.

The fully restored Johnson log cabin includes exhibits of what life was like in the 1860s, such as a reconstructed kitchen, bedroom, and storage area. The site also includes an outdoor fire ring that may have been used during the summer months to keep from overheating the cabin.

The National Park Service replaced old fencing throughout the Johnson Settlement, using traditional cedar rails and posts. Today visitors to Lyndon B. Johnson National Historical Park may tour the Johnson Settlement, following a self-guided nature trail that leads from the visitor center to the Provost-Johnson log cabin, the Bruckner barn, and the cooler house and barn that were built by James Polk Johnson. A gravel trail and lane leads past pens and pastures that feature prized Texas longhorn cattle.

Volunteers dressed in period costumes reenact pioneer life of the late 1860s.

Judge N. T. Stubbs, a son-in-law of James Polk Johnson, built the well house and used it for storage. The well house and other small outbuildings have been restored at the Johnson Settlement to provide visitors with a traditional setting of pioneer life in the Texas Hill Country.

LBJ touches the wall of his grandparents' log cabin, likely remembering the many stories he was told as a child of pioneer life in the Texas Hill Country.

The front porch of the Provost-Johnson log cabin had fallen into disrepair but was still intact in the early 1970s.

Historical studies reveal that the Johnson Settlement did not have a blacksmith shop on the property but likely had a blacksmith travel to the site for necessary repairs. Here a volunteer actor demonstrates blacksmith techniques used in the late 1860s.

Period actors use a bit of humor to demonstrate that a pioneer woman's work is never done.

Lyndon Johnson, center, holds daughter Lynda as the family visits the log cabin in 1946, prior to its restoration. Lady Bird Johnson is on the far right, and LBJ's sister Rebekah Baines Johnson is second from the left next to uncle Barry Roebuck (left) and uncle Tom Johnson (second from right).

Visitors have the opportunity to walk through the Johnson Settlement and experience the pioneer spirit at the German-style Bruckner barn. Exhibits located throughout the settlement serve as a testament to the courage and resolve of Lyndon Johnson's pioneer ancestors.

Two

The Johnson City Community

There is no other place that can do for me what this land, this water,
these people, these hills, and these surroundings can do.

—Lyndon Baines Johnson

For 10 years, James Polk Johnson, nephew of LBJ's grandfather, was the owner of the Johnson Ranch on Town Creek, the site of present-day Johnson City. The area, known today as the "crossroads to the Texas Hill Country," has a long history as a crossroads. Settlers traversed a north-south route from the town of Blanco to the Colorado River as early as Spanish times. Explorer Bernardo de Miranda passed this way, crossing the Pedernales in the vicinity of Johnson City on his way to inspect the supposed silver deposits near Packsaddle Mountain near what is now Llano County. Travel by horse or horse and wagon had long established this section of the Pedernales Valley as a natural stopping place and crossroads to San Antonio, Austin, and settlements to the west and north. McCarty Spring, located just 4 miles to the northwest of Johnson City, was a favored way station for travelers between Austin and Fredericksburg. Andrew Jackson Johnson, an older brother to Tom and Sam Johnson, located his home near this spring in 1858 or 1859. But these crossroads sites were nothing more than small settlements or ranching operations.

James Polk Johnson made the transition from rancher to businessman very successfully. It was his organizational ability that converted what had been a natural way station into a settled community and eventually the county seat. Johnson City—which for many years was mainly a ranch trade center—had a steady tourist business from its origins. The population fluctuated from 400 in 1925 to 950 in the late 1940s and today is just fewer than 1,200 residents. Johnson City continues to be mainly a tourist center, with numerous state and local parks within a few miles of the community. Lyndon B. Johnson National Historical Park is a main attraction.

Johnson City was named after James Polk Johnson, nephew to Lyndon Johnson's grandfather, Sam Ealy Johnson Sr. By the middle to late 1870s, the nearest post office, mill, and general store were located 14 miles south of Johnson Ranch in the town of Blanco, located in southern Blanco County. Settlers in the north end of the county, including James Polk Johnson, began to plan for a town near the northern area and attempted several times to get the county seat moved from Blanco to a more centrally located area of Blanco County.

Education in Blanco County began with one-room schoolhouses. The school system grew slowly, as many of the young men who attended seem to have dropped out at an early age, possibly to work on family farms or ranches. This photograph of a group of unidentified children was taken at the Buffalo School, located between Johnson City and Sandy, Texas, some time in the 1890s.

Horse-and-buggy was the main mode of transportation in the early 1900s.

A group of unidentified Johnson City residents enjoys a picnic in the Texas Hill Country, similar to the barbecue and picnic held in 1879, when the future of Johnson City was decided. In 1879, the Johnson Ranch hosted a barbecue held at the springs on Town Creek. The chair of the meeting announced that the purpose of the assembly was to plat a proposed town. Three sites for a town were offered, including a site on Flat Creek, about 1.5 miles west of the meeting site, owned by Capt. Rufe Perry. A three-man committee rode out to each proposed site and returned by 3:00 p.m. to report on each location prior to a vote. The site accepted by vote of the settlers was a 320-acre plot of land on the Pedernales River offered by James Polk Johnson. After the decision, friends hoisted James up on their shoulders and cheered him for his victory and for the decision by the residents to name the new town after him.

James Polk Johnson surveyed Johnson City to allow for a public square. He was optimistic that the county seat would eventually be relocated to Johnson City. The square was laid out to eventually house the Blanco County Courthouse. It took another 11 years and several hotly contested votes before Johnson City became the Blanco County seat. In the meantime, the town was platted, and James began to sell lots in the newly founded Johnson City. He donated lots for schools. A post office was established, and the community began to thrive. The local newspaper, the *Record-Courier*, which continues in business today, was established in 1883.

Businesses began to grow and prosper in Johnson City at the turn of the century. This photograph was taken around 1900.

James Polk Johnson built and operated a steam-powered cotton gin and gristmill on Town Creek, taking in and milling corn and cotton, the principal crops of the area. This gin was purchased by George Crofts in the 1940s and converted to a milling and grain operation that flourished until the late 1970s. The gristmill is adjacent to the Johnson Settlement at the Lyndon B. Johnson National Historical Park. Since closing as a gristmill in the 1970s, the structure has housed a variety of businesses, including a restaurant, bar, and shop.

Cotton was known as "white gold" in Texas and throughout the South. A group of unidentified workers stack a loading dock with cotton bales.

By the time of his premature death at age 40 in 1885, James Polk Johnson had built the Pearl Hotel—named after his daughter—and had another building under construction that was to be a general merchandise store. The Pearl, located on the town square across from the Blanco County Courthouse, continues to operate as a guesthouse and tea parlor. It was renamed the Adams Hotel in 1929 but now retains its original name.

The James Polk Johnson building, constructed in 1885 by Lyndon B. Johnson's second cousin, housed the town's first jail in its basement and served as the first Johnson City Courthouse. The building was also a temporary home for Johnson City's first church congregation, a group of Methodists, who met in an upstairs room until their church was constructed. Later Lyndon B. Johnson had his local offices in this building. The James Polk Johnson building is now home to Johnson City Bank, which was established in 1906. According to tax records, the bank held $10,220 in deposits by the end of its first year in business.

Crosby-Russell owned the Johnson City mercantile business in the late 1890s. The building later became the Withers and Spauldings mercantile and now serves as the Johnson City Chamber of Commerce and a satellite visitor center for Lyndon B. Johnson National Historical Park. The building has been renovated to look like it did in the 1915–1920 era. It includes a general store exhibit as well as exhibits spanning Lyndon Johnson's campaigns, when the building was used as a gathering place in the 1960s.

The Withers and Spauldings building was a general mercantile that served as a gathering point for farmers bringing their turkeys to market. It was also used as a meeting place to discuss news of the day and politics. Sam Ealy Johnson Jr., Lyndon B. Johnson's father, was a local and state politician who frequently participated in political conversations, and his eldest son enjoyed watching and learning from those discussions. Sam Jr. is seen here in 1913 wearing his favorite white Stetson hat as he poses on the boardwalk.

A crowd gathers in the streets of Johnson City for a Prohibition parade around 1915. During this time, the Texas Legislature was being influenced by the Anti-Saloon League. Sam Johnson Jr. refused to be influenced by lobbyists and voted against Prohibition. Despite not attending church as frequently as would have satisfied his fundamentalist constituents, Sam Jr. served five terms in the Texas House of Representatives as a Populist Democrat.

Around 1908, a group of men proudly show off their motorcycles. Today Johnson City is a favorite stopping point for motorcyclists who enjoy riding in the Texas Hill Country.

E. P. Ross Hardware Store was one of the many bustling businesses in Johnson City in the early 1900s.

Though its new status as the county seat boosted the economy of the community, Johnson City did not get modern utilities until the 1930s, when Representative Lyndon Baines Johnson sponsored legislation that introduced full electric power to the area under the Lower Colorado River Authority and the Pedernales Electric Cooperative. This scene is a glance down the town's Nugent Street after electricity poles and wires were in place.

Lyndon B. Johnson Memorial Hospital was built in 1968. The building is now used as the headquarters and visitor center of the Lyndon B. Johnson National Historic Park.

The Blanco County Courthouse was constructed in 1916. During the Great Depression, farm and ranch values plummeted and crop production fell. The number of farms in the county continued to drop; by 1940, only 632 farms remained in Blanco County. The effects of the Depression on the county were tempered by a marked rise in government projects in the area, many of them acquired through the influence of Lyndon Baines Johnson, who had developed a close relationship with Pres. Franklin D. Roosevelt. Many of the county's roads were paved, and the federal government's Civilian Conservation Corps worked to improve state parks in the area. Though many county residents suffered through the years of the Depression, these projects help to explain a rise in the population of Blanco County between 1929 and 1940. By 1940, the county's population was 4,264.

With a shovel in hand, Lynda Johnson helps plant a tree in Johnson City's town square on April 5, 1966. She and Lady Bird Johnson planted six oak trees in town in a ceremony honoring their grandparents.

Three

THE BIRTHPLACE

A president's hardest task is not to do what is right, but to know what is right. Yet the presidency brings no special gift of prophecy or foresight. You take an oath, step into an office, and must help to guide a great democracy. The answer was waiting for me in the land where I was born.

—Lyndon Baines Johnson

Lyndon Johnson's birthplace was reconstructed on its original foundation in 1964 based on old photographs and LBJ's fond memories of the house. The president hired J. Roy White, a well-known architect from Austin, Texas, to begin a modest restoration of the reconstructed Samuel Ealy Johnson farmhouse. White and his staff contacted neighbors and Johnson family members for information regarding the birthplace. According to White's notes and final report on the reconstruction, much of the information that influenced his work was acquired by reading the book *The Johnson Family Album*, written by Lyndon's mother, Rebekah Baines Johnson.

LBJ's birthplace sits on a 2-acre tract along the Pedernales River adjoining LBJ Ranch near Stonewall, Texas. The first recorded owner of the land was Rachel Means, who secured a patent on what was known as Survey No. 6, from the Republic of Texas signed by Pres. Anson Jones on April 30, 1845. In 1882, Samuel Ealy Johnson Sr. and Eliza Bunton Johnson—LBJ's paternal grandparents—purchased 950 acres of the patent. Over the years, the Johnsons built homes, barns, and other structures on the property, including the home that would become LBJ's birthplace. In the early 1900s, they built and moved another home on the property.

At the time of Lyndon's birth, the Austin-Fredericksburg road paralleled the north bank of the Pedernales River, passing in front of the Johnson home. When traveling to and from the nearby towns of Stonewall, Hye, and Johnson City, the Johnsons forded the Pedernales River at a crossing near the Johnson Cemetery, located between the LBJ Ranch homestead where grandparents Sam Sr. and Eliza lived and the home that is now known as the Birthplace.

The Johnson family poses in front of what would later become Sam Ealy and Rebekah Johnson's first home, the birthplace of Lyndon Baines Johnson, near Stonewall, Texas, around 1897. Pictured, from left to right, are Tom Jesse Johnson (LBJ's great uncle), Jessie Johnson Hatcher, Jane McIntosh Bunton, Eliza Bunton Johnson (LBJ's paternal grandmother), Sam Johnson Sr. (LBJ's paternal grandfather), Kate Johnson Martin, Lucia Johnson Price, Frank Johnson Martin, T. J. Martin, and George Desha Johnson.

Samuel Ealy Johnson Sr., left, and Eliza Bunton Johnson, fourth from left, built and lived for many years in what is now known as the Birthplace. Here they pose with unidentified friends and family in front of the home around 1900. LBJ's father, Samuel Johnson Jr.—also known as "Little Sam"—moved into the house shortly after 1905. Two years later, in August 1907, he brought his bride, Rebekah Baines Johnson, to the house on the Pedernales River. As a welcoming gift for her, Sam Jr. had painted the house bright yellow. One year later, on August 27, 1908, Lyndon Baines Johnson was born.

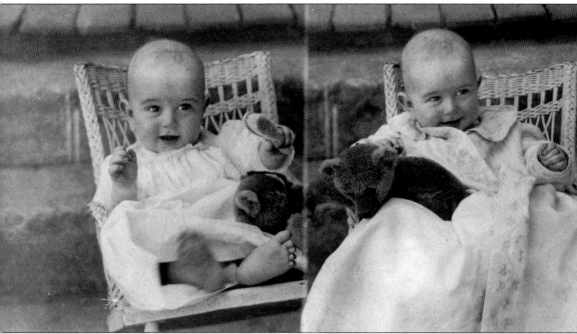

This is supposedly the first photograph of baby LBJ at age six months in early 1909 at his birthplace home. It was taken with a stereo camera that was adapted to place two different exposures side by side on a single negative. Lyndon's mother penned an account of his birth in her book titled *The Johnsons*. She wrote, "It was daybreak, Thursday, August 27, 1908, on the Sam Johnson farm on the Pedernales River near Stonewall, Gillespie County. In the rambling old farmhouse of the young Sam Johnsons, lamps burned all night. Now the light came in from the east, bringing a deep stillness, a stillness so profound and so pervasive that it seemed as if the earth itself were listening. And then there came a sharp and compelling cry—the most awesome, happiest sound known to human ears—the cry of a newborn baby; the first child of Sam Ealy and Rebekah Johnson was discovering America."

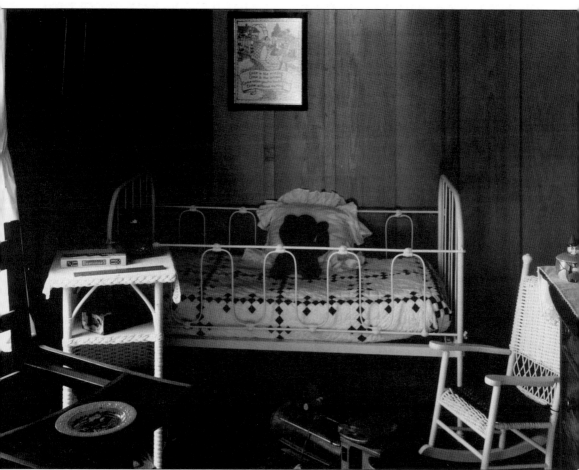

A framed quote from Rebekah's account of Lyndon's birth now hangs in the east bedroom of the reconstructed LBJ Birthplace. During his many guided tours of the home, President Johnson pointed out the framed quote, proudly letting his guests know that his mother wrote it. Lyndon Johnson's nursery was carefully reconstructed with as many heirlooms as possible, including a china clown dish on the dresser. This dish was a Christmas gift that four-year-old Lyndon bought for his aunt Lucie. He was so excited about the present that he gave it to her three weeks early, declaring, "it cost me a whole dime and it's worth every penny!"

Baby Lyndon poses in the Birthplace yard wearing cousin Thomas Jefferson Martin's hat around 1909.

As a child, Lyndon walked to the nearby one-room Junction School, where his mother first enrolled him at age four. Rebekah was a firm believer in the power of education. Rebekah, "Little Sam," and their growing family lived in the home on the Pedernales River until 1913. In April 1965, Pres. Lyndon Johnson visited the building that provided his first schoolhouse experiences.

Rebekah Baines Johnson is pictured 1917. Rebekah's parents taught her to read at a very early age. Reading was always one of her life's greatest pleasures, and she passed this love of reading and education on to her children. When Lyndon was two years old, she used wooden blocks etched with letters to teach him the alphabet. Like his mother, Lyndon learned to read at a very young age. Many years later, as President Johnson participated in tours of the Birthplace, he acknowledged the powerful influence of his mother, proudly highlighting the fact that she was able to attend Baylor College at a time when few women received a higher education.

Located just a quarter of a mile east of the Birthplace is the Junction School, the one-room schoolhouse where young Lyndon was enrolled at age four. It opened on November 21, 1910. Sixty-two years later, the National Park Foundation acquired the property as part of the Lyndon B. Johnson National Historical Park.

More than 60 years after Lyndon Johnson attended the Junction School, the 36th president of the United States used the Junction School as the site of his signing of the Federal Aid to Education Act on April 11, 1965. This was the first general aid-to-education program ever adopted by Congress, and it provided programs to help educate disadvantaged children in city slums and rural areas, such as the area where Johnson was born and raised. President Johnson invited his first schoolteacher, Kate Deadrich Loney, to join him for the signing on April 11, 1965.

Our old home
Stonewall Texas

LBJ's paternal grandparents lived near what is now the LBJ Birthplace. Pictured from left to right are Sam Jr. and Rebekah Johnson (LBJ's parents), Sam Sr. and Eliza Johnson (LBJ's grandparents), and three unknown guests in front of Sam and Eliza's house near Stonewall, Texas, around 1910.

Sam Jr. and Rebekah lived intermittently at the Birthplace and at the boyhood homes until the Birthplace property was sold in 1922. The original house was torn down in the 1940s. Pieces of the original home were used to construct a smaller house located near the birth site. These materials, in turn, were used whenever possible during the Birthplace reconstruction, including pieces of the original limestone fireplace. The reconstructed house represents how Lyndon Johnson wanted us to see his birthplace. It was reconstructed and furnished using old photographs and the president's fond memories.

A young Lyndon Johnson sits on the porch with his sister Josefa Hermine Johnson around 1915. After two more children were born to the Johnson family, "Little Sam" moved the household to nearby Johnson City, to the house that is now known as the Boyhood Home. Sam Sr. and Eliza Johnson continued to live on the property adjacent to the Birthplace. Young LBJ returned to the property many times to visit. After their deaths in 1915 and 1917, respectively, the Johnson heirs sold a portion of the remaining property to Samuel Ealy Johnson Jr. at the price of $19,500 for 433.68 acres. LBJ's younger brother, Sam Houston Johnson, reportedly said, "It was too much money for the land and Daddy never did do too well."

Here Lyndon was born in the west bedroom with the fireplace and windows shaded by a tree.

This undated drawing, created by family member Mary Johnson, was included in *The Johnson Family Album*. Architect Roy White and his team followed the original board and batten construction and also included the open hallway or dogtrot breezeway in the center of the house that was designed to provide ventilation in hot weather. Lyndon Johnson's birthplace has the distinction of being the only presidential birthplace reconstructed, refurbished, and interpreted by an incumbent president.

Lyndon Johnson poses for a portrait at age 18 months.

Lyndon Johnson often told stories about how his mother tolled the bell at the back of the house to bring his father and the farm hands in from the fields for dinner. Upon completion of the Birthplace restoration, architect White wrote in his final report, "The Birthplace could not have been accomplished without knowing that the encouragement of the First Lady was always in the background. Her feeling for the correct things and for precise detail was a continual and stimulating influence. . . . Always present, too, was the remembrance of Mrs. Rebekah Baines Johnson, whose book was a constant inspiration to perfect as nearly as possible the proper restoration of the house." White ended his report by stating, "So may this reconstructed home in which her first son was born continue as a tribute to her faith and to her love for her family."

President Johnson uses the antique telephone at the Birthplace.

Lyndon Johnson would often sit on the porch and ask, "Did you ever see anything more comfortable than this?" Here, he enjoys the Birthplace porch with White House secretaries Vicky McCammon, left, and Marie Fehmer, right. Architect White's wish that the Birthplace serve as a tribute was recognized immediately upon the July 10, 1966, public opening of the house, when 1,205 people went on the inaugural-day tours. Although open only limited hours for 19 days during the summer months, there were 14,225 visitors in 1966 and 31,439 in 1968. President Johnson enjoyed showing visitors his birthplace.

As President Johnson led visitors onto the back porch of his birthplace, he often took hold of the pump handle and demonstrated its action. Here, he tells U.S. Secretary of Labor Williard Wirtz, left, and U.S. Secretary of Commerce Luther Hodges, right, the story of his earliest memory of his mother, when he was about four years old. He recalled that he was standing beside his mother as she pumped a bucket of water from the cistern. "Darkness was approaching and mother was crying," Johnson recalled. "I asked her why and she said because she was afraid to be alone at night so far out in the country." He mentioned that it was cotton-picking season and his father was late getting home. "I looked at mother and said, 'Don't worry Mother, I'll take care of you.'"

Four

THE BOYHOOD HOME

*I know from personal experience that abiding values and abundant
visions are learned in the homes of our people.*

—Lyndon Baines Johnson

Lyndon Johnson was five years old when his family moved from his birthplace to what is now known as the Boyhood Home, located on Ninth Street in Johnson City, one block from the present-day National Park Service Visitor Center. By the time of the move, Lyndon had two younger sisters, Rebekah and Josefa. One year after the move, in 1914, Sam Houston was born in the Johnson City home, followed two years later by Lucia Huffman.

The Johnson house was a warm, active residence, with frequent sleepover parties with cousins and the neighborhood children. Lanterns were strung up in the yard and children gathered to play games. At Easter, there was always an egg hunt at the Johnson home, and at Halloween there was an annual party with a variety of games to entertain both children and adults. Christmas was always the highlight of the year, with lots of homemade goodies and many festive activities leading up to the Christmas Day celebration.

The warm and welcoming atmosphere of the Johnson family home is preserved in the Boyhood Home. Family members helped to collect furniture, pictures, books, knickknacks, and family heirlooms, enabling visitors to get a feel for and broad understanding of the family's life between 1913 and 1937.

Four of the Johnson children pose on the lawn of the Boyhood Home around 1914. Pictured from left to right are Josefa Hermine, Rebekah Luruth, Sam Houston, and Lyndon Baines.

Pictured are the five Johnson children in 1921. From left to right are Lucia, Josefa, Rebekah, Lyndon, and Sam. Just prior to this photograph being taken, Lyndon reportedly received his first pair of long trousers, a sure sign of growing up.

Young Lyndon Johnson stands near the family car in front of the Boyhood Home in 1915.

The Boyhood Home is pictured as it appeared prior to renovation. The family moved from the Boyhood Home back to Lyndon's birthplace from 1920 to 1922. During this time, Lyndon stayed with extended family members so that he could continue his high school studies. Thirty-two months later, the family returned to the Ninth Street home and continued to live there for eight more years, welcoming friends and family, political colleagues, and business partners. Rebekah was known for "setting a good table," and the dinner table was usually at full occupancy with last-minute guests.

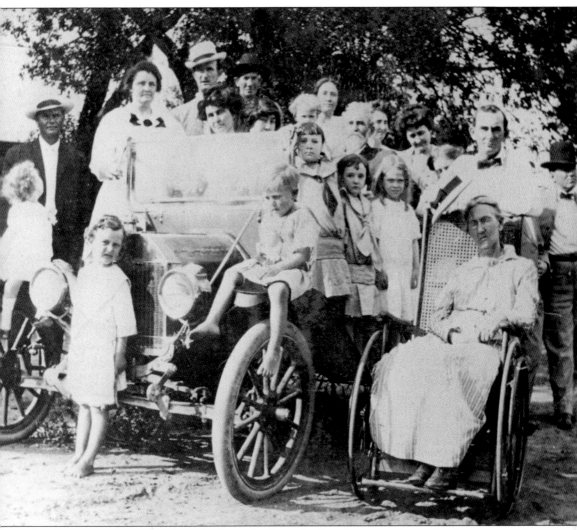

Lyndon, at age five or six, leans back on the front fender of a car, posing with a large group of unidentified cousins, aunts, and uncles. His father, Sam Jr., is the tallest man in the white hat, standing behind the windshield. His mother, Rebekah, is standing in front of her husband. Lyndon's grandmother Eliza Bunton Johnson is seated in the wheelchair. This photograph was taken in 1913 or 1914.

Lyndon's cousin, Ava Johnson Cox, poses at the back gate of the Boyhood Home.

This photograph shows one of the back buildings of the Boyhood Home complex.

Lyndon Johnson relaxes in a rocking chair on the porch of a Boyhood Home back building. Other people on the April 11, 1965, tour are Ann Brinkley (walking), David Brinkley (standing with his back to the camera), Chester Loney (taking a seat), and Kate Deadrich Loney, LBJ's first schoolteacher.

An unusual snowstorm hit the Texas Hill Country on Christmas Day, 1926. Lyndon and his friends and siblings enjoy a rare snowball fight in the yard of the Boyhood Home.

The front porch of the Boyhood Home is where the Johnson children spent time playing, sleeping on a hot summer night, or standing in the corner for a punishment. Lyndon's sister, Lucia Johnson Alexander, recalled that the porch was referred to as "the crying gallery." It was where a child had to remain until he or she quit laughing, crying, or otherwise.

Lyndon Johnson's high school graduation photograph was taken in front of the Boyhood Home in 1924, when he was 15 years old. He once stated, "My Daddy and my dear Mother were equally affectionate, equally considerate with their children and we responded in kind. When I was not prepared with my studies, Daddy and Mother both stayed up with me until they were satisfied that I had mastered the assigned subject. I looked at them with equal respect and cherish them with identical love." Both of Lyndon's parents were educated and well read. They passed along a love of learning to their children. Lyndon's father, Sam Ealy Johnson Jr., was known to have spur-of-the-moment spelling bees and debates that he said made children think on their feet.

As a teenager, Lyndon Johnson enjoyed playing baseball. This 1923 photograph shows him as the catcher with an unidentified batter.

Rebekah Baines Johnson was active in the Johnson City Parent Teacher Association as well as community theater and other local activities. She also taught elocution from the Ninth Street Home. For a period of time, Rebekah and her husband, Sam Jr., operated the local newspaper, the *Blanco County Record*, often working from home. Sam Jr. was involved in local and state politics and often brought home both work and political colleagues. The central hall of the Boyhood Home features Sam Jr.'s rolltop desk and matching swivel armchair that he used for his home office, with Rebekah acting as his secretary.

In *The Johnson Family Album*, Rebekah wrote an evaluation of her husband Sam Ealy Johnson Jr.'s political endeavors: "He was ambitious not so much for his own success as for that of his friends and children, being alert to the interests of a loved one and persistent in his promotion of the same. In his own advancement, he was retiring and modest. . . . Highly organized, sensitive, and nervous, he was impatient of inefficiency and ineptitude and quick to voice his displeasure; equally quick, however, in making amends when some word of his caused pain to another. . . . He was intensely loyal and generous far beyond his means. His faith in a real and personal Heavenly Father was strong. To those who knew him best, great-heart seems best to describe him."

Sam Ealy Johnson Jr. works at his desk in the Texas House of Representatives in 1905.

The Boyhood Home displays many of Sam Jr.'s political accomplishments, including the Alamo Purchase Bill—which saved the historic site from the wrecking ball—as well as farm appropriations and rural education bills, themes that Lyndon Johnson later echoed during his own political career as a member of the U.S. House of Representatives, senator, vice president, and president of the United States. Lyndon launches his own political career from the porch of the Boyhood Home as his mother, Rebekah, and his wife, Claudia "Lady Bird" Alta Taylor Johnson, sit behind him for support. In a 1937 special election, his parents had the honor of voting for their son when he was elected to his first term in the U.S. House of Representatives.

This Johnson family portrait was taken at the Boyhood Home on November 28, 1968, with, from left to right, Lyndon Johnson, grandson Patrick Lyndon Nugent, Luci Johnson, Lynda Johnson Robb, and Lady Bird Johnson.

The LBJ Boyhood Home was designated as part of the Lyndon B. Johnson National Historical Site. Lyndon's younger brother, Sam Houston Johnson, is seated on the Boyhood Home porch during a dedication ceremony.

The National Park Service sign marks the Boyhood Home. Lyndon's father died on October 23, 1937. Five years later, wanting to ensure that the Ninth Street home remained in the family, Rebekah Baines Johnson sold the property to Lyndon for $10. He assumed responsibility for the mortgage and taxes while his mother continued to live in the house. Rebekah Baines Johnson proudly witnessed her eldest son be elected to the U.S. Senate and to the position of Democratic Majority Leader in 1955. She died on September 12, 1958, before seeing him elected as vice president and president. Lyndon had the house remodeled in 1964. One year later, it was deeded to the board of trustees of the Johnson City Foundation. Following the establishment of the Lyndon B. Johnson National Historic Site by the 90th Congress on December 2, 1969, the foundation deeded the property to the United States for $1 on January 15, 1970.

The park staff members who unveiled the historical marker are, from left to right, superintendent Harry O'Bryant, Roy Byars, and Luke Kent.

Lyndon Johnson talks with Blanco County resident Roy Byars prior to the dedication ceremony at the Boyhood Home.

Lyndon Johnson and U.S. Navy admiral William Raborn relax on the Boyhood Home porch swing on April 11, 1965.

Five

THE LBJ RANCH AND TEXAS WHITE HOUSE

The Texas Hill Country is where people know when you are sick, love you while you are alive, and miss you when you die.

—Lyndon Baines Johnson

The present-day LBJ Ranch includes the Texas White House complex, the runway and hangar, LBJ's show barn, the Junction Schoolhouse, the LBJ Birthplace, the Johnson family's private cemetery, and the final residence of LBJ's grandparents, Sam Ealy Johnson Sr. and Eliza Bunton Johnson.

The ranch is rich with family history and its enduring pioneer spirit. The Hereford cattle that roam the pastures are descendants of LBJ's prized herd and are reminders of his cattle drover grandfather, Sam Sr., and great uncle, Thomas Jesse Johnson.

Sam Sr. died on February 25, 1915, and Eliza passed away on November 30, 1917. The Johnson farm had several heirs who agreed to sell the 433.68 acres to Sam Jr. for $19,500. Sam Jr. moved his family back to the farm for a few years, but he was deeply in debt and decided in 1922 to sell off sections of land. By the end of that year, the Johnson farm had passed out of the family until the 1960s, when land was reacquired by Lyndon Johnson.

LBJ's aunt Frank and her husband, Judge Clarence Martin, owned the home that is now known as the Texas White House. Lyndon Johnson often described his memories of the home: "I first came to this house as a very young boy. This was the big house on the river. My uncle and aunt lived here. They would always ask all the in-laws to come here and spend their Christmas. Frequently, I would come here during the summer when Judge Martin, my uncle, lived here and I'd spend three months' vacation from school riding with him and looking after the cattle. I kept coming back to this house. I guess I must have had a yearning to some day own it. But when we came here on one of the periodic visits in 1952, my aunt told me that she was in advancing years and poor health and she wondered if I wouldn't buy the place. And I did." Lyndon Johnson spent Christmas 1951 with, from left to right, aunt Frank Barnett Johnson Martin, uncle Thomas Jesse Johnson, aunt Ava Johnson, and aunt Jessie Hermine Johnson.

A German immigrant named William "Polecat" Meier built the original native limestone residence in 1894. Lyndon's aunt and uncle purchased the Meier home in 1909 and enlarged it, incorporating the original stone house into the ranch home. LBJ bought the home from his aunt Frank in 1951 to keep it in the family.

The Johnson family spent Christmas 1952 at the LBJ Ranch. Pictured from left to right, Lady Bird, Luci, Lynda, and Senator Lyndon Johnson wish everyone a Merry Christmas from the front lawn. The LBJ Ranch house is the centerpiece of the ranch. Lady Bird Johnson called it the family "heart's home" that housed a family of children and grandchildren, ranch workers, and their families and was a respite for numerous friends, guests, world leaders, and diplomats from the time Lyndon and Lady Bird Johnson purchased the property in 1951 until her death in 2007.

During a press conference on the front lawn of the ranch house, Lady Bird Johnson stands in the background, shooting a motion picture film of the event as U.S. House of Representatives Speaker Sam Rayburn (left), Senator Lyndon Johnson, and Adlai Stevenson (right) talk with the media. During LBJ's presidency, news correspondents covering meetings and press conferences on the ranch first described the ranch house as the Texas White House. The name stuck.

President Johnson sits with members of the German press on the Texas White House lawn on July 8, 1967, joined by sportscaster and former Dallas Cowboys football player Drew Pearson (second from left with the mustache).

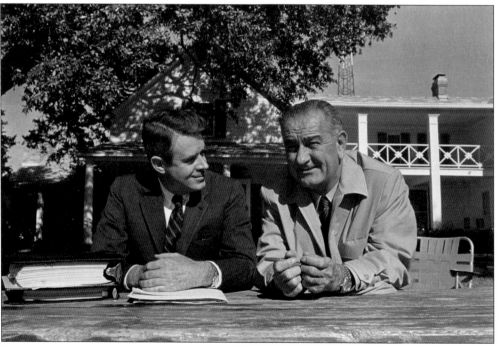

Pres. Lyndon Johnson holds a meeting on the lawn of the Texas White House with Deputy Secretary of Defense Cyrus Vance on December 22, 1964.

The house, front yard, roadways, pastures, and groves of oak trees along the Pedernales River provided President Johnson with a familiar and comfortable environment while holding press conferences and meetings, overseeing the federal government, and carrying the full weight of the office of the president on his shoulders. Johnson takes a peaceful moment to lean on a tree branch and enjoy the view of the LBJ Ranch as he contemplates the difficult issues of the day on July 5, 1968.

The lawn of the Texas White House was a popular place for meetings, barbecues, or just a peaceful moment of relaxation.

President Johnson and Secretary Robert McNamara hold a meeting on the lawn at the LBJ Ranch on December 22, 1968.

Dignitaries visiting the LBJ Ranch were encouraged to leave a memento by signing the paver stones that line the walkways around the Texas White House. Inscribed signatures of Stew Udall and Bob McNamara are pictured above. Visitors to the LBJ Ranch have an opportunity to walk along the pathways to view a host of dignitaries that left their "John Hancock" behind.

Visitors to the Texas White House may take a guided tour through the house, including the living room where the Johnson family held both private and public events. Above, President Johnson utilizes the living room to meet with state governors on December 21, 1966. Seated from left to right, facing the camera, are Gov. Richard Hughes, President Johnson, Marvin Watson, and Gov. Farris Bryant.

Technological advancements in the 1960s allowed the president to operate almost exactly as he could from the Oval Office. The 6,400-foot LBJ Ranch airstrip received and dispatched the "Washington shuttle," which provided daily connections with Washington, D.C., in order to ferry mail, top-secret communiqués, and government officials to and from the ranch. Pictured above, President Johnson talks with guests onboard the Jetstar airplane.

President Johnson drives his favorite Cushman golf cart to transport visitors from the Jetstar to the Texas White House.

President Johnson and Lady Bird Johnson bid farewell to the beagles on May 31, 1965, as they walk down the airstrip toward the Jetstar to depart from the LBJ Ranch.

This aerial view of the LBJ Ranch shows the Jetstar parked at the hangar, located near the Texas White House. Today the Jetstar sits near this exact spot, on display since mid-2010. The hangar now serves as a visitor center, gift shop, and exhibit hall. It is also used for special events held by the Friends of LBJ National Park, a private, nonprofit organization dedicated to promoting public support for the care and preservation of Lyndon B. Johnson National Historical Park.

In November 1963, the ranch had two telephone lines and a television antenna tower. By early 1964, there were 70 telephone lines, a microwave communications system, a 360-foot radio tower capable of reaching several states, a fully staffed switchboard, and a military detail at the ready with helicopters and airplanes on stand-by. Pictured above, President Johnson and Gen. William Westmoreland drive the Cushman golf cart onto the airstrip as a helicopter lands in the distance.

The white-faced Herefords of the LBJ Ranch graze near the airstrip on July 4, 1968, oblivious to the airplane and helicopter waiting for Pres. Lyndon Johnson.

Throughout Lyndon and Lady Bird Johnson's public life, they invited the world to dine, visit, relax, meet, and consult on the issues of the day while enjoying the peace and beauty of the Texas Hill Country. The ranch staff prepares for a barbecue on April 1, 1967, by grilling steaks on an open flame pit. President Johnson stands in line for barbecue with Guillermo Sevilla-Sacasa and Nellie Connally during the Latin American Ambassadors Weekend at LBJ Ranch.

President Johnson practices roping calves at the LBJ Ranch on November 20, 1965.

One of LBJ's favorite modes of transportation around the ranch was his antique fire truck. Visitors to the LBJ Ranch have an opportunity to view the fire truck and several other presidential vehicles that are stored in the hangar.

Dam and Spillway at L. B. J. Ranch

This 1960s-vintage postcard shows the spillway on the Pedernales River at the LBJ Ranch.

Lady Bird Johnson and Senator Johnson make a stop on the Pedernales River spillway as they cruise around the LBJ Ranch in a 1934 Ford Phaeton in December 1959.

As a teenager, Lyndon Johnson spent time on his uncle Clarence and aunt Frank Martin's cattle ranch, which is now the LBJ Ranch. No ranch tour is complete without gazing at the prize Hereford cattle that roam the ranch or stopping by the show barn on the property.

The Pedernales River cuts through the LBJ Ranch, providing a peaceful view in all directions.

From left to right, Senator Lyndon Johnson, Lynda Bird Johnson, Lady Bird Johnson, and Walter Jenkins pose on the Johnson dam and low-water crossing on the Pedernales River at the LBJ Ranch in September 1954.

Lady Bird Johnson relaxes on rock on April 16, 1965, enjoying a hike through the Texas Hill Country terrain of the LBJ Ranch.

Lady Bird Johnson sits in a field of wildflowers on the LBJ Ranch on May 10, 1990.

Built in Germany from 1961 to 1968, the Amphicar is the only civilian amphibious passenger automobile ever to be mass produced. A total of 3,878 vehicles were produced in four colors: Beach White, Regatta Red, Fjord Green (Aqua), and Lagoon Blue—the color of President Johnson's Amphicar, which is on display in the LBJ Ranch hangar. President Johnson enjoyed surprising unsuspecting guests when taking them for a ride in his Amphicar. Joseph Califano Jr. once said, "The President, with his secretary Vicky McCammon in the seat alongside him and me in the back, was driving around in his small blue car with the top down. We reached a steep incline and the car started rolling rapidly toward the water. The President shouted, 'The brakes don't work! The brakes won't hold! We're going in! We're going under!' The car splashed into the water. I started to get out. Just then the car leveled and I realized we were in an Amphicar. The President laughed. As we putted around the water, he teased me, saying 'Vicky, did you see what Joe did? He didn't give a damn about his President. He just wanted to save his own skin and get out of the car.' Then he'd roar with laughter."

President Johnson's office at the Texas White House served many purposes: a presidential office, meeting place, and the center of both personal and official events. Visitors today may tour the office and view many of the original furnishings and decor from the 1960s. Pictured above, President Johnson, seated, hefts a gift as Lady Bird Johnson, other staff, family, and close friends watch him open birthday presents on August 27, 1966.

Senator Lyndon Johnson and Lady Bird Johnson, both wearing western clothing and cowboy hats, pose in front of the living room fireplace in the LBJ Ranch house in September 1959. While at the ranch, they both enjoyed living a comfortable, casual lifestyle. After a tour of the Texas White House, visitors often comment on the relaxed atmosphere and family ambiance expressed in the furnishings and decor.

President Johnson meets with White House Press Secretary Bill Moyers, left, and Special Assistant to the President Jack Valenti, right, in the president's office at the Texas White House.

President Johnson's office has been renovated to appear as it did in the 1960s, including original furnishings and his personal belongs. The office opened to the public for the first time on August 27, 2008, on Lyndon Johnson's 100th birthday.

President Johnson takes time from his busy schedule to enjoy his grandson, Patrick Lyndon Nugent, on January 6, 1968. The president and his dog Yuki sing to Patrick in the dining room of the Texas White House.

Senator Lyndon Johnson and Lady Bird Johnson pose in a grove of trees as they relax on the LBJ Ranch in 1951.

President Johnson and Lady Bird Johnson discuss the issues of the day as they walk through a field of Texas wildflowers on the LBJ Ranch on July 5, 1968. Lady Bird's interest in conservation awareness and beautification influenced the Highway Beautification Act of 1965, which is still in effect today. Later in life, she was instrumental in founding the Lady Bird Johnson Wildflower Center in Austin. The facility is open to the public and is now an Organized Research Unit of the University of Texas at Austin.

Pres. Lyndon Johnson sits on a fence on the LBJ Ranch, posing with his dog Yuki on December 29, 1967.

The Lady Bird Wildflower Center is located in Austin about an hour from the LBJ Ranch. Lady Bird's love for Texas wildflowers that flourished during her time on the ranch culminated in the 1982 dedication of the Wildflower Center in her honor. Lynda Johnson Robb, left, and Luci Johnson, center, accompanied Mrs. Johnson to the dedication ceremony.

This aerial view of the LBJ Ranch was taken on June 24, 1967. The view looks west toward the ranch. The Pedernales River and Ranch Road 1 are on the left. Visitors to the LBJ Ranch take Ranch Road 1 from Highway 290 when traveling to the ranch from the National Park Service Visitor Center in Johnson City.

Looking north, this aerial view shows the expansive pastures of the LBJ Ranch. Visitors to the ranch are now able to drive onto the property, circle the airstrip and show barn, and park near the Texas White House and hangar.

From 1951, when the Johnsons purchased the house from Lyndon's aunt Frank Martin, through Lady Bird's death in 2007, the Johnsons liked to say that "all the world was welcome" to LBJ Ranch. The LBJ Ranch and Texas White House hosted visiting dignitaries and at least one Pakistani camel driver that Vice President Johnson invited to visit during an international goodwill tour. The house and grounds with its sprawling live oak trees witnessed the joys of the presidency as well as the misery and human toll the office demands of all who hold it. Lady Bird Johnson and Pres. Lyndon Johnson welcome German chancellor Ludwig Ehrhard (second from right) to the Texas White House on December 28, 1963. The unidentified man on the right may be a German diplomat or interpreter.

Vice president-elect Lyndon Johnson and president-elect John F. Kennedy greet a large crowd of supporters during a trip to the LBJ Ranch on November 16 and 17, 1960. The team had won the presidential election on November 5, 1960.

President-elect John F. Kennedy smiles during an informal interview at the LBJ Ranch as vice president-elect Lyndon Johnson looks on from behind. The photograph was taken during a November 1960 trip to the ranch.

Pres. Lyndon Johnson meets on December 22, 1964, with the Joint Chiefs of Staff around the picnic table on the LBJ Ranch front lawn. Pictured, clockwise, are president Lyndon Johnson, Secretary of Defense Robert McNamara, Maj. Gen. Chester Clifton, Gen. Curtis LeMay, Gen. Earle Wheeler, Deputy Secretary of Defense Cyrus Vance, Gen. Harold Johnson, Adm. David McDonald, and Gen. Wallace Greene.

Coretta Scott King visits the LBJ Ranch for a September 19, 1979, conversation with Lady Bird Johnson.

Pres. Lyndon Johnson and vice president-elect Hubert H. Humphrey are photographed on horseback during a trip to the LBJ Ranch on November 2, 1964.

Lady Bird Johnson often spoke of Lyndon Johnson's generosity, his need to be surrounded by people, and his strong desire to make life better for Americans. Certainly the influences of his heritage, upbringing, and life experiences in and around LBJ Ranch molded the character and drive of a man who had a vision for a greater country. Lyndon Johnson completed his circle of life when he was buried in the Johnson Family Cemetery, located just across the ranch driveway from the LBJ Birthplace on the LBJ Ranch. After his death, Lady Bird Johnson continued to live part-time at the ranch. Below, she poses at the front gate of the Texas White House on June 1, 1991.

Pres. Lyndon B. Johnson enjoyed the life of a rancher during his post-presidency years, while reflecting on his vast political career. He coined the phrase the "Great Society" in a 1964 speech at the University of Michigan, and it became the umbrella policy of his administration that included some of the most sweeping civil, environmental, health, education, and societal laws in U.S. history. Johnson's War on Poverty and Aid to Education laws surely sprang from the experiences of his youth. The heritage of his cattle drover and ranching ancestors, his love of the land, and the beauty of the Texas Hill Country, as well as the influences of Lady Bird Johnson, served as motivation for the Clean Water Act, the Clean Air Act, and the designation of more national park sites than any U.S. president in history.

Today the National Park Service—with great assistance from the Friends of LBJ National Park, the LBJ Library and Museum, the Western National Parks Association, the Texas Parks and Wildlife Department, the Lady Bird Johnson Wildflower Center, former members of the Johnson administration, and, of course, the Johnson family—is preserving and caring for these places once owned by the 36th president and his loving wife, Lady Bird Johnson. On September 30, 1967, President Johnson and Lady Bird Johnson relax on a bench near the Pedernales River on the LBJ Ranch as their dog Yuki sits nearby.

Six

THE PARK

All the world is welcome here.

—Lyndon Baines Johnson

Lyndon B. Johnson National Historical Park is the premier location to experience the environment that shaped the character, public policy, and continuing legacy of the 36th president of the United States. The National Park Service is dedicated to preserving and interpreting the rich collection of resources that illuminate and clarify Lyndon B. Johnson. The staff is also dedicated to enhancing regional and national awareness and providing an understanding of a complex and compelling figure in the history of the American presidency.

The park was established on December 2, 1969, as a National Historic Site "In order to preserve in public ownership historically significant properties associated with the life of Lyndon B. Johnson." It was renamed a National Historical Park in December 1980. The original historic site included the Reconstructed Birthplace on the LBJ Ranch near Stonewall and the Boyhood Home in Johnson City.

The original visitor center for the Lyndon B. Johnson National Historical Park was located in the Birge Alexander House, which was once owned by the president's sister and her husband. In 1975, park statistics show that 403,427 people visited Lyndon B. Johnson National Historical Park. Since 2001, the park averages more than 100,000 registered visitors each year. Those numbers have increased with the opening of LBJ Ranch following Lady Bird Johnson's death in 2007 and the renovation of the Texas White House to illustrate what it looked like in the 1960s, during Lyndon Johnson's years as 36th president of the United States.

President Johnson poses near the Alexander House with his sister, Lucia Johnson Alexander, on January 4, 1964.

Lyndon Johnson and Lady Bird Johnson meet with Interior Secretary Stewart Lee Udall, center, in the Texas White House office in 1972 to discuss plans for Lyndon B. Johnson National Historical Park.

The Lyndon B. Johnson National Historical Park Visitor Center is nestled in a grove of trees located on Lady Bird Lane in Johnson City, across the road from the LBJ Boyhood Home.

The Johnson Settlement
is a short walk from
the center. The park
is part of the National
Park Service.

Tourists relax on the banks of the Pedernales River on the LBJ Ranch as a tour bus is seen in the background.

This unidentified female bus driver provided one of the first tours of the LBJ Ranch. In the photograph below, cattle from the LBJ herd are seen on one side of the Pedernales River as another tour bus drives past the local church to bring more visitors to the LBJ Ranch.

The Friends of Lyndon B. Johnson National Historical Park works in partnership with the National Park Service to provide educational and interpretive programs. A variety of public events are also held throughout the year, including a barbecue at the ranch and the annual "Timeless Christmas" festivities, where visitors can experience an 1860s-era Christmas at the Johnson Settlement, with period decorations of a simple tree and lighting from lanterns, candlelight, and the fireplace. Visitors may stroll over to the Boyhood Home to experience a 1920s-style Christmas. During the summer months, park staff hosts "Movies Under the Stars" at the LBJ Ranch, where visitors, friends, and families can enjoy a picnic and watch movies under the stars, just as Lyndon Johnson and his family did with friends and visitors in the hangar. The Johnson Settlement offers an event center available for weddings, family reunions, and other special events. Visit the Lyndon B. Johnson National Historical Park Web site at www.nps.gov/lyjo/ or visit the Friends of LBJ National Park Web site at www.friendsoflbjnationalpark.org for information on events or to book an event at the Johnson Settlement.

Family and friends gather for a wreath-laying ceremony every year on August 27, Lyndon Johnson's birthday. On the president's 75th birthday in 1983, his grandson, Lyn Nugent, laid the wreath, attended by, from left to right, Patrick Nugent, Rebekah Nugent, Claudia Nugent, and Lady Bird Johnson.

Luci Johnson leads the annual LBJ 100 Bicycle Ride, held in late March. During the bicycle tour, Luci takes a group of riders to featured places on the LBJ Ranch, including the Johnson Family Cemetery, the LBJ Birthplace, and the Texas White House to tell personal stories of her father, Lyndon Baines Johnson, and his "full circle of life" heritage depicted throughout the ranch.

The Lyndon B. Johnson National Historical Park would not be possible without the generosity of Lady Bird Johnson and Lyndon Johnson, pictured above on the LBJ Ranch on December 31, 1972, less than one month before President Johnson's death on January 22, 1973. Their gracious gift of family land and assets incorporates more structures and history significant to the entire life of an American president than any other presidential site in America. The Johnson family, especially daughters Lynda and Luci, help the National Park Service depict an accurate representation of life in the Texas White House in the 1960s. Lyndon Johnson's wish was that the park as a whole, and especially the LBJ Ranch, "not become a sterile relic of the past" but rather use events and activities to continue to educate and invigorate visitors through the years ahead.

www.arcadiapublishing.com

Discover books about the town where you grew up, the cities where your friends and families live, the town where your parents met, or even that retirement spot you've been dreaming about. Our Web site provides history lovers with exclusive deals, advanced notification about new titles, e-mail alerts of author events, and much more.

MADE IN THE USA

Arcadia Publishing, the leading local history publisher in the United States, is committed to making history accessible and meaningful through publishing books that celebrate and preserve the heritage of America's people and places. Consistent with our mission to preserve history on a local level, this book was printed in South Carolina on American-made paper and manufactured entirely in the United States.

This book carries the accredited Forest Stewardship Council (FSC) label and is printed on 100 percent FSC-certified paper. Products carrying the FSC label are independently certified to assure consumers that they come from forests that are managed to meet the social, economic, and ecological needs of present and future generations.

FSC
Mixed Sources
Product group from well-managed forests and other controlled sources

Cert no. SW-COC-001530
www.fsc.org
© 1996 Forest Stewardship Council

Find Your Place in History.